Written by Jean-Pierre Reymond
Illustrated by Luc Favreau

Specialist adviser:
Chris Rees, London Butterfly House

173660

ISBN 1 85103 114 6
First published 1991 in the United Kingdom
by Moonlight Publishing Ltd,
36 Stratford Road, London W8
Translated by Sue Birchenall

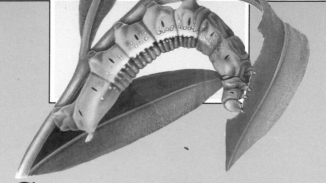

Caterpillars, Butterflies and Moths

Do you know how many
different kinds of butterflies
and moths there are?

There are more than a hundred thousand different kinds of butterflies and moths. They live all over the world, from the frozen wastes of Siberia to the tropical rain forests. They form a special class of insects called Lepidoptera, or 'scale-wings', because of the tiny scales which cover their wings in exquisite patterns.

There are four stages in the life of a butterfly or moth: the egg, the caterpillar, the chrysalis, and finally the adult. Many butterflies and moths spend three-quarters of their lives as caterpillars. For a very long time, people thought caterpillars were a completely different species.

Male butterflies and day-flying moths recognize a female by the colour of her wings.

This bright yellow butterfly, a male Birch Swallowtail from North America, has spotted a brown-winged female.

Once they find each other, the butterflies mate, and remain coupled together for hours.

Male and female butterflies and moths are often very different.

The colours of the female are usually more subdued. The male's wings are brightly coloured so that the female will recognize him as he flies towards her – as long as she knows who he is, she won't turn him away!

The male and female Emperor Moth aren't much alike at all.

Night-flying moths recognize females by their smell. A male can scent a female from a distance of several kilometres, and flits through the darkness to find her hiding among the leaves. They mate together for some hours, before the male flies off again, and the female sets about finding a suitable place to lay her eggs.

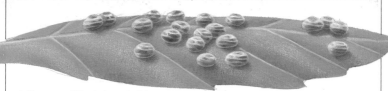

A Lappet Moth has laid her eggs on this leaf.

Some moths and butterflies just lay their eggs as they fly along, and hope for the best.
Most are careful, though, and choose a spot where the newly-hatched caterpillars will find food. Many lay their eggs on plants which they recognize by smell and know are good to eat.

Eggs come in all sorts of shapes, sizes and colours. They vary according to the species.

The number of eggs a female lays also depends on her species, but it can be anything between 25 and 10,000. The eggs are very tough, and can survive temperatures of $-40°C$.

The Emperor Moth lays her eggs in a bracelet round a twig.

European Map butterfly eggs look like strings of beads hanging below a leaf.

A Scarce Swallowtail caterpillar
struggles out of its egg.

When the caterpillar is ready to hatch,
it chews a hole in the shell with its tiny
jaws so that it can wriggle out of the egg.
It finishes off the rest of the eggshell, and
then sets about doing some serious eating.
Caterpillars eat all the time.

The warmer the weather, the faster they
grow; caterpillars which live in groups
inside cosy silken nests grow at a quite
spectacular speed.

Monarch caterpillar

Garden Tiger Moth caterpillar

Morpho caterpillar

Charaxes caterpillar

Privet Hawkmoth caterpillar

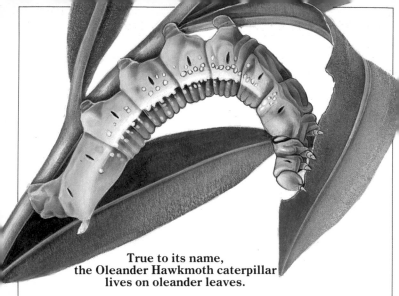

True to its name,
the Oleander Hawkmoth caterpillar
lives on oleander leaves.

Most caterpillars feed on plants. You
may have noticed holes in leaves where
caterpillars have been feeding.
Many eat only one sort of plant all their
lives.

A few caterpillars live in tree-trunks, or in
the horns or hooves of animals. But there
isn't much to feed on there, so those
caterpillars can only grow very slowly.

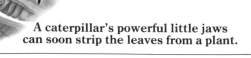

A caterpillar's powerful little jaws
can soon strip the leaves from a plant.

A caterpillar eats so much that eventually it becomes too fat to fit inside its skin, so it swells up the front part of its body until the old skin splits and the caterpillar can wriggle out of it. This is called moulting.

Most caterpillars only shed their skins about five times, but some have as many as seventeen moults!

The new skin is crumpled, damp and pale, but it soon hardens and quickly regains its colours.

It sometimes takes a long time to wriggle out of the old skin, so caterpillars usually hide away to moult, out of sight of their enemies.

The Clothes Moth caterpillar feeds on wool. If it can't find much to eat, the caterpillar may take up to three years to grow into a moth. But with lots of woolly jumpers to feed on, it's ready in only four weeks!

The Honeycomb Moth caterpillar lives on beeswax.

This Swallowtail caterpillar is much too big for its old skin!

This Swallowtail caterpillar is much too big for its old skin!

When it is ready to moult, the caterpillar waits without moving –

it even stops eating! Most caterpillars spin a silken pad attached to a leaf or twig, and cling to it as they shed their skin. Caterpillars which live underwater wrap themselves in a silky waterproof blanket under a water-lily leaf, so that they can breathe the oxygen released by the plant. Once the caterpillar is full-grown, it is time for it to become a chrysalis.

Caterpillars begin their preparations for the chrysalis stage by finding a suitable place. This chrysalis is safe in a burrow hollowed out underground by the caterpillar.

As it prepares for its final moult, the caterpillar changes colour and grows thinner. This time, when the old skin is shed, the caterpillar disappears; **the chrysalis,** or pupa, emerges, and remains there, not moving, not feeding, until the butterfly is formed. This can take anything from eight days to four years, depending on the species and the climate.

A Gypsy Moth caterpillar changes into a chrysalis.

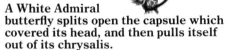

A White Admiral
butterfly splits open the capsule which
covered its head, and then pulls itself
out of its chrysalis.

As it struggles free from its chrysalis, the new butterfly or moth can't yet spread its beautiful wings. First it has to contract its muscles, so that blood can begin to circulate through the tiny veins; gradually the limp, damp wings expand, and are held open until they have dried and hardened. As the wings spread for the first time, tiny reddish drips rain down from them – the waste from the caterpillar's last meal. In the Middle Ages, when swarms of Painted Ladies emerged together from the chrysalis, people used to think that it was raining blood!

Every butterfly and moth has six legs, two pairs of wings covered in scales, and two antennae. Nearly all feed through a long sucking-tube called a proboscis, which they keep rolled up inside their heads when they aren't feeding.

Most butterflies and moths live on nectar, the sweet liquid secreted by flowers. They suck it up through their proboscis.

Convolvulus Hawkmoth

The length of the proboscis varies according to the depth of the flowers the butterfly usually feeds from.

Six-spot Burnet Moths feeding

Some species of Hawkmoth feed without settling, hovering above the flower, their wings beating so fast that you cannot see them. Most butterflies and moths only live for a month or two, though those which hibernate may survive for up to nine months. Some species without a proboscis never feed; their lives are very short.

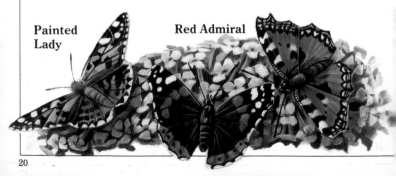

Painted Lady

Red Admiral

Large Blue

Pearl-bordered Fritillary

The antennae of butterflies and moths are far more sensitive than our noses.

They can pick up minute particles of scent which we would never notice, and the slightest trace is enough to guide them to the flowers they like to feed on. Butterflies and moths need flowers, but sometimes flowers need them too. The yucca plant, which grows in Central America, could not survive without the little Yucca Moth, which uses its specially curved proboscis to fertilize the yucca flowers.

The Giant Birdwing, one of the largest of all butterflies, lives in the jungle of New Guinea.

Camouflage artists... Lizards and birds, snakes and monkeys like nothing better than a tasty moth or a juicy caterpillar. To protect themselves, moths, butterflies and caterpillars have developed such superb camouflage that their enemies find them impossible to spot; they look like leaves, thorns, twigs, animal droppings, spiders, hornets – even snakes!

Some butterflies and moths look exactly like dead leaves.

1 Kallima butterfly, from Asia
2 Convolvulus Hawkmoth caterpillar
3 Peppered Moth caterpillar
4 Purple Emperor chrysalis
5 Bombyx terrifica caterpillar
6 Female Brimstone butterfly
7 Black Hairstreak chrysalis
8 Lappet Moth
9 Death's-head Hawkmoth
10 Poplar Hawkmoth caterpillar

The eye-spots behind its head make this harmless caterpillar look alarmingly like a wide-eyed snake.

Instead of blending into the background,

some species confuse or scare off their predators by their ocelli, or eye-spots, circular markings which look just like huge eyes. When the Eyed Hawkmoth on the right opens its wings suddenly, the startling sight of its eye-spots is quite enough to scare away a hungry thrush!

Owl butterflies have wing-markings which look unnervingly like feathers round the large, unblinking eyes of a predatory owl.

When a Puss Moth caterpillar is disturbed, it puffs up the front part of its body, pushes out two red threads from its forked tail, and waves them like whips over its head. It looks just like a miniature dragon.

The hornet and bee above are actually a Hornet Clearwing Moth and a Bee Hawkmoth!

Butterflies and moths are very important to the environment. They help to pollinate flowers so that they can grow into fruit and vegetables.

Caterpillars can sometimes be a nuisance, though. Processionary caterpillars, which live in nests in oak or pine trees, are very destructive. At sunset the procession of about five hundred caterpillars, in twos and threes, emerges from the nest and sets about devouring the foliage of a tree. By dawn, it is stripped bare. People trying to protect the forest have to be careful not to touch the caterpillars, which are covered with poisonous hairs that give you a painful rash. But other caterpillars are very useful. Long ago, the Chinese discovered that the silkworm weaves its cocoon out of a single thread of silk, which can be unravelled and woven into beautiful fabrics.

A Silk Moth emerges from its cocoon.

Graphium pylades

Morpho

Africa

Heliconius
burneyi

**South
America**

sard

Agrias
narcissus

**Venezuela,
Surinam**

**Colombia,
Ecuador,
Peru**

Papilio paeon

Ornithopter

ris (male)

Colombia, Central America

Papilio alcmenor

Agrias
apalus

Northern
India

Upper
Amazon

Catagramma
peristera

Bolivia

New Guinea

radisea (male)

Prepona
omphale

Brazil

29

This crab-spider has paralysed a Small Pearl-bordered Fritillary, and is now sucking out its blood.

An ichneumon, or parasitic wasp, crawls from a Swallowtail chrysalis. The wasp grub ate the contents before pupating.

Ants carry the Large Blue caterpillar to their nest to milk the sweet liquid it produces.

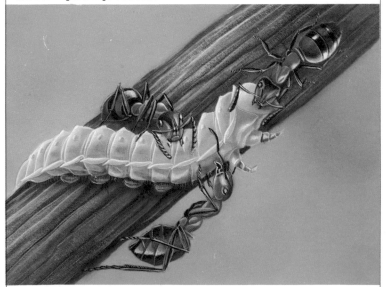

Carnivorous red ants attack and eat other insects, including this unfortunate caterpillar.

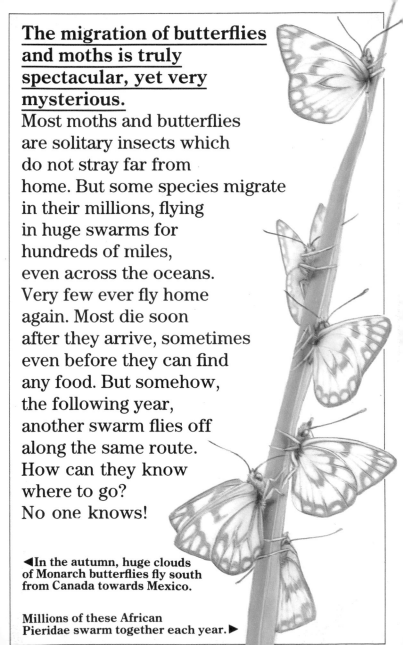

The migration of butterflies and moths is truly spectacular, yet very mysterious.

Most moths and butterflies are solitary insects which do not stray far from home. But some species migrate in their millions, flying in huge swarms for hundreds of miles, even across the oceans. Very few ever fly home again. Most die soon after they arrive, sometimes even before they can find any food. But somehow, the following year, another swarm flies off along the same route. How can they know where to go? No one knows!

◀In the autumn, huge clouds of Monarch butterflies fly south from Canada towards Mexico.

Millions of these African Pieridae swarm together each year. ▶

33

How many different butterflies can you see on these two pages?

Does it look like twelve? Actually there are only six – each one is shown on this page with its wings folded, and opposite with them spread. Can you manage to match up the pairs?

1 and d = Orange-tip
2 and a = Purple Emperor
3 and b = Comma
4 and e = Heliconius antiochus
5 and c = Morpha menelaus
6 and f = Grayling

35

Index

antennae, 21
Birch Swallowtail, 8
birth of butterfly, 18
breathing, 16
camouflage, 22
caterpillar, 7, 12, 14,
   15–17, 23
chrysalis or pupa, 7, 17, 18
Clothes Moth, 15, 16
difference between male
   and female, 9
egg, 7, 9, 11
Emperor Moth, 9, 11

enemies, 22
environmental benefits, 26
European Map butterfly, 11
eye-spots, 24
feeding, 12, 14, 15
Fritillary, 21, 29
Giant Birdwing, 21
Gypsy Moth, 17
hatching, 12
hibernation, 20
Lappet Moth, 11
Lepidoptera, 6
mating, 8, 9

migration, 32
moulting, 15, 17
nectar, 20
nesting, 12
night-flying moth, 9
ocelli, 24
Oleander Hawkmoth, 14
Owl butterfly, 24
Painted Lady, 18
pollination, 26
predators, 22
proboscis, 18, 20, 21

processionary
  caterpillar, 26
Puss Moth, 24
rainforest, 6
Red Admiral, 20
Scarce Swallowtail, 12
scent, 9, 11
Siberia, 6
silkworm, 26
White Admiral, 18
wings, 18
Yucca Moth, 21